I Love Pink!

(A Trans Tale)

By Trina Casey
Illustrated by Mari Nkomo

This Real Life Books

Copyright © 2019 Trina Casey

All rights reserved

ISJN: 978-9-0 83-01710-5

For Harper and other World Changers:

I wrote this book for all the kids who struggle in a society that doesn't want to accept them, but they find the strength to love themselves anyway!

It's for all the kids bullied and told they are not enough because they shine so brightly that others can't see! It's for the kids that don't get the protection they deserve but they still manage to stand up and protect others! These young warriors will be the positive change in the world!

For helpful tips on how to use this book turn to page 31. There you will find questions to explore this story with your child.

Hello! My name is Juanita, and I really love ME!

I'm super duper in love with the color PINK!

Pink has been my favorite color for as long as I can remember, which isn't that long since I turned 6 last December!

Mommy and Daddy let me always be the best of me,

No matter how hard that sometimes can be.

I love ALL of my family except for my great uncle, Bert.

He's not very kind to me and looks at me with a smirk.

Just because my body doesn't fit how I feel inside,

it's really not a reason for friendship to be denied.

"Isn't that RIDICULOUS?"

"Ridiculous" is a big word Daddy taught me when I was only two.

I say it when people say things to me that are not nice or even true!

He tells me, "Don't care what they think and be true to you!"

And that is precisely what I intend to do.

Daddy told me to stand up tall, put my proudest face on and say,

"That's RIDICULOUS!" Then just calmly walk away.

I do my best to hide the hurt I feel inside,

but some days it hurts so much all I can do is cry.

One day at school, I was wearing my favorite pink bow in my hair.

Jeremiah pulled it out and yelled at me,

"That's not something you should wear!"

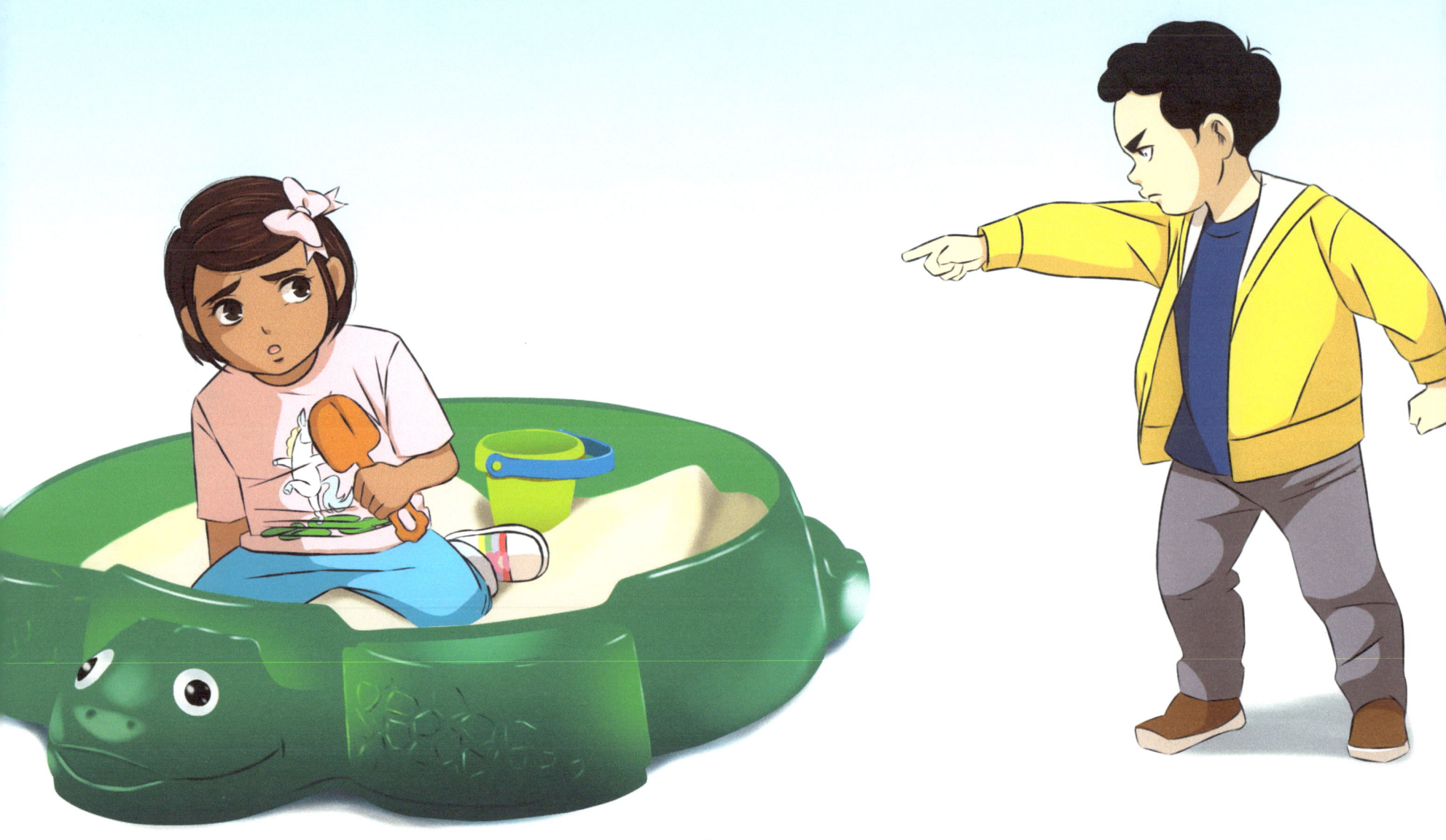

Then I asked him, "What's your favorite color?"

In a really nasty voice, he said, "Blue!"

So I smiled and said, "Would you be happier if I wore that color too?"

He told me, "You're a boy, not a girl, act like it!"

I did not like what he said, NOT ONE BIT!

I stood up tall and proud and said,

the first thing that popped into my head!

Then Miss Wilkerson saved me as she always does.

She is the sweetest teacher ever and always shows me love!

She made Jeremiah apologize and said to him with real stern eyes,

"Leave Juanita alone and try to be more civilized!"

She picked up my favorite bow and placed it gently back in my hair.

I really appreciate how Miss Wilkerson shows me that she cares.

I used to get picked on almost every day,

when I asked the girls in the class, "Can I play?"

But they would be mean to me and say, "Oh, just go away!"

When I'd try to play with the boys,

they would bully me and take away all my toys.

Many days I played by myself until Kiana became my friend.

We promised to stick together through everything, thick and thin.

One thing I love about Kiana is she lets me be me!

She never bullies or is unkind, with her, I feel free!

I really love how she thinks!

Oh, did I mention her favorite color is also PINK?

She stands up for me when the other kids are mean.

Kiana and I really do make an EXCELLENT team!

The days Kiana didn't come to school were absolutely the worst!

I'd ask her, "Are we still friends, and she'd say, Yes, of course!"

One day Kiana came to school with a really big black eye.

I asked her how it happened, and all she did was cry.

I put my arms around her and said, "I'll take care of you."

I really want to help her because that's what friends should do.

I told Mommy and Daddy about Kiana's black eye.

They said they would look into it and gave a sad sigh.

They said that life can be hard and sometimes isn't always fair.

I told them that she was often hungry at lunch, so I would always share.

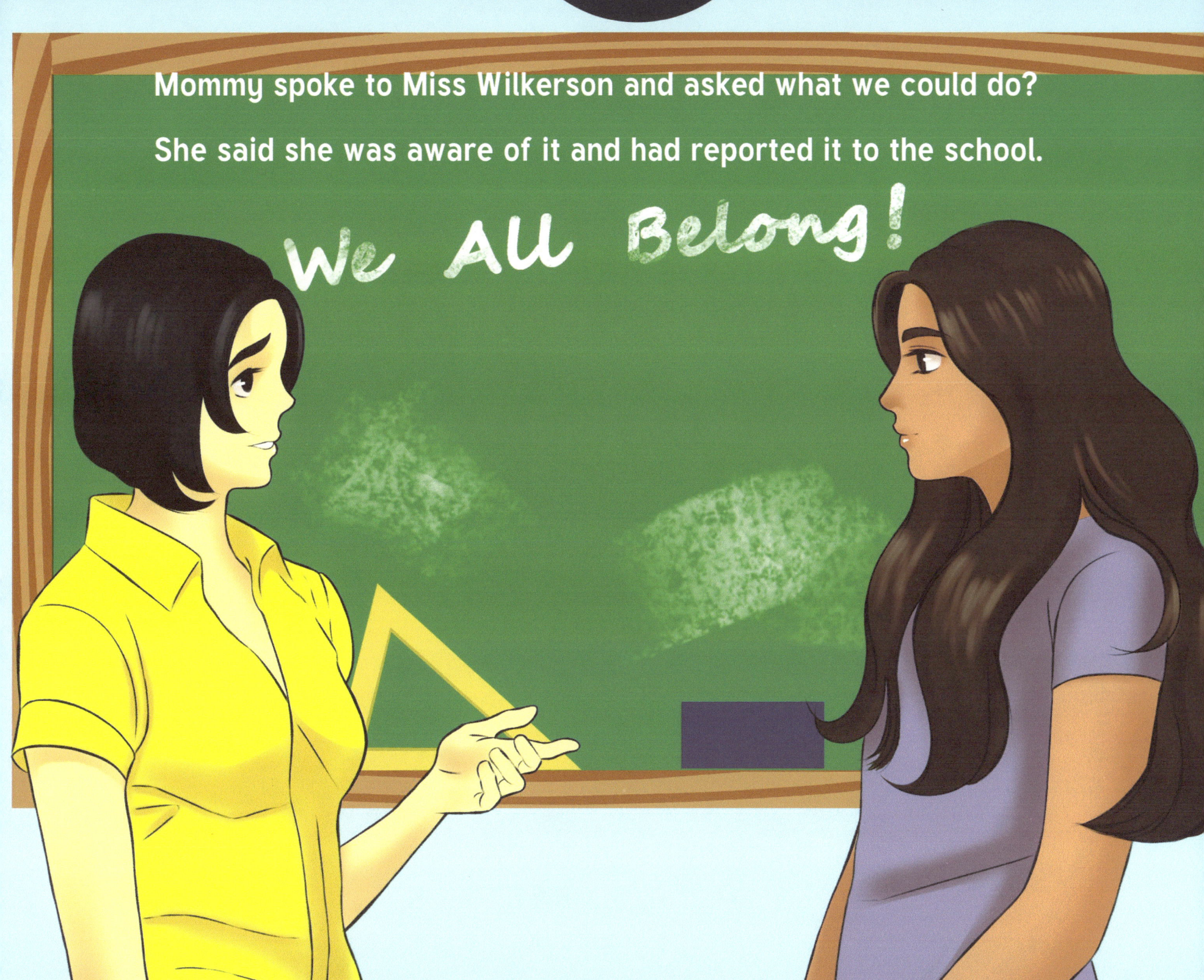

Mommy said that we would foster Kiana and give her some loving care,

because we had a lot of space and so much love to share.

A few days later, Kiana came to school with a trash bag full of clothes.

Mommy took it from her, bent down, and spoke to her softly nose to nose.

"I know Kiana that there's a lot you've been going through,

but we would love it if you'd stay with us. If that's ok with you?"

Kiana wrapped her arms around Mommy's neck and made some crying sounds.

It was so funny I blew green snot from my nose,

then I jumped up from the ground and made a silly pose!

Parent Notes

Dear Parents, Teachers, Caretakers, and World Changers,

I wrote, **"I Love Pink! (A Trans Tale)"** with the LGBTQ community in mind. As more and more research and analysis comes out confirming that gender identity is not a choice but something you are born with, I feel it is essential that young children who are struggling to understand the body they are in get the love and support they need.

It can be difficult for other children to understand their LGBTQ brothers and sisters. This story is for them. It is also for those parents looking for ways to explain to their children that being different is not a bad thing. I also tackle the sensitive subject of child abuse and hope children will use their voices to expose their abuse and the abuse of others. You will find some helpful questions to discuss gender identity and child abuse. Also, I don't write necessarily with age in mind because I believe children have innate wisdom. Take this time to teach your child vocabulary to deepen the educational experience. If they ask for the meaning of words, it means they are engaged, which is what you want! Reading with your child is a bonding experience, and they want to learn from you.

Juanita is the brave and confident Latin trans person who wants the world to accept her. Luckily for Juanita, she has parents that support her journey with love and build strong confidence in her identity. Pointing this out to your child is essential. They need to know even if some people will not accept them others will. Some voices will speak up for them and there are those that will speak down to them. Just remember more people are on your side than against you! There is more good in the world than bad! You belong!

Question: Have you ever felt like you don't belong?

The girls have a difficult time understanding transgender identification as well as the boys. Girls are programmed by society that they must separate themselves from the opposite sex. Though this is changing, historically girls were told dolls and "feminine" activities were the best for them. We need to challenge these stereotypes to have a more inclusive and equal society. Girls are not limited to dolls and pink. When we teach them these biases, we restrict their ability to be confident and supportive of the LGBTQ community. They may even feel threatened as well and kick them out of the playhouse. That's not very nice, is it?

Question: Would you not play with someone just because they are different from you?

The boys/Jeremiah represent the societal voice that assaults and even physically harms the LGBTQ community. There has been an aggressive stance that tries to stop transgender peoples' confidence from developing. Teaching our little boys that it's okay to like pink doesn't mean they will be gay. It normalizes that it's okay if others do like pink or may be gay. It is just a color and signifies nothing but a preference which is personal. So let boys like pink, dolls, and or anything else that has been placed in the "girl" category. It's about exploration. They will choose the path they want as adults. Give them space to explore who they are.

Question: Do you ever feel embarrassed about liking dolls and are teased for liking "girl" things or liking race cars and "boy" things?

Kiana plays a beautiful yet painful role in the story. Kiana is the little brown/black girl who stands up for Juanita because she too is put down by society. This oppression is a common theme in many other cultures as well. Brown/black children who are abused by society are generally the ones who stand up for the oppressed because they live with oppression every day. Kiana comes from a stressful and abusive environment. I don't go into much detail of her backstory mainly because the circumstances vary so much.

Abuse is a learned behavior just as love. As a historically abused group, brown/black people have been taught violence through brutality, so I choose not to demonize a group who have already been unfairly treated. I do want to show how abuse affects the self-esteem of children but also how much love can turn that around. Kiana and Juanita embrace each other and protect each other. Imagine what a beautiful world we would have if we all did this.

I also wanted to point out the trash bag Kiana carries her belongings in. Children of color have higher instances of being placed in the foster care system. This bag reduces their sense of dignity. It's a dream for them to be put into loving homes. Quite often, they are placed in a home where they are further abused or even abused for the first time. The foster care system needs an overhaul and a lot more resources.

Question: What would you do if you knew your friend was being hurt or was hungry every day?

Miss Wilkerson has one of the most critical careers on the planet! Our children are at school more than they are at home and teachers have a multi-faceted role. They are educators not only in academics but how to be in the world socially. It is vital that teachers are educated in SEL (Social Emotional Learning). Miss Wilkerson appropriately and immediately intervenes regardless of her personal beliefs around transgender identity. Teachers must keep their own views at home, or they may harm a child. Even well-intentioned teachers have to know how to teach with neutrality. This means all kids of all colors and genders are children first and deserve love and acceptance. Teachers help mold the minds of the next generation. They need to be educated and paid according to that importance. I think most people become teachers because they love children. They need to be able to do this without the financial burden put on them globally. Pay them more, and they will have more of themselves to give to our children. Educate them well in Emotional Intelligence, and they will help our children make this world equitable and empathetic.
Question: Do you feel heard by your teacher when you ask for help?

LOVE

www.ingramcontent.com/pod-product-compliance
Lightning Source LLC
Chambersburg PA
CBHW050848010526
44107CB00017BA/1211